Preface

حَدِيثاً بَعَثَهُ اللهُ يَوْمَ الْقِيَّامَةِ فَقيهاً عالِماً

Prophet Muḥammad (s): Whoever from my nation memo[rizes forty ḥadīth... Allah will raise on] the Day of Judgment as a learned scholar.

Dear Parents and Educators,

Alḥamdulillah, Kisa Kids is pleased and humbled to announce the launch of *40 Ḥadīth for Children*, a book dedicated to helping children memorize 40 ḥadīth on various akhlāqī topics. The hope is for this book to help children come closer to mirroring the lives of the beloved Ahl al-Bayt. The hearts and minds of children are pure and impressionable; thus, we should make the most of this precious time in their lives by planting the seed of the teachings of the Ahl al-Bayt in their hearts, and pray that this seed will bloom as they grow older.

Inshāʾ Allāh by instilling a deep love and understanding of the lives of the Ahl al-Bayt in our children from an early age, they will form a connection to this holy family and take practical steps to follow in their footsteps and teachings. For this book, we have chosen simple aḥadīth centered on many different topics, such as hygiene, nutrition, friendship, akhlāq, and spirituality, to demonstrate to our children that the Ahl al-Bayt are not just our guides in spiritual affairs; rather, they are our guides in all aspects of life.

Learning aḥadīth from the Ahl al-Bayt that provide guidance on everyday matters, such as brushing one's teeth, will encourage children to engage in such actions while fostering a practical connection to them. By studying these sayings, children will also increase their *maʿrifah* (deep understanding) of these role models and the teachings of Islām in general. As they grow into young adults, inshāʾAllah this well-developed relationship and connection will serve as a guide for them in their everyday and long-term decisions.

This is our humble approach, and we welcome all feedback. If you have any ideas or suggestions on how we can improve our methods, are an interested educator, or feel that you can creatively contribute to these efforts, please contact us at info@kisakids.org. Al-Kisa Foundation is a nonprofit organization that creates educational material for future generations with the goal of strengthening their knowledge and connection to Islām and the Ahl al-Bayt. Our work thrives through your support and donations, so any type of assistance you can provide, such as time, feedback, skills, or anything else, is greatly appreciated and will be rewarded by Allāh, inshāʾAllah.

With Duʿās,
Nabi R. Mir (Abidi)

TABLE OF CONTENTS

Children and Akhlaq 6
   Jealousy 8
   Kindness 10
   Respecting Parents & Teachers 12
   Honesty 14
   Stubbornness 16

Children and Behavior 18
   Mistakes 20
   Rushing 22
   Trying Our Best 24
   Doing Good Deeds 26
   Trustworthiness 28

Children and Manners 30
   Reputation of Muslims 32
   Forgiving Others 34
   Removing Dislike 36
   Showing Love 38
   Keeping Good Friends 40

Children and Guests 42
   Guests and Angels 44
   Serving Guests 46
   Respecting Guests 48
   Making Room for Others 50
   Whispering 52

Children and Hygiene 54
   Washing Your Hands 56
   Brushing Our Teeth 58
   Oversleeping 60
   Messiness 62
   Washing Clothes 64

Children and Nutrition 66
   Feeding the Needy 68
   Eating Less 70
   Chewing Properly 72
   Eating Hot Food 74
   Protecting the Environment 76

Children and Spirituality 78
   Helping the Oppressed 80
   Blessings from Allah 82
   Success 84
   Humility 86
   Good Children 88

Children and Upbringing... 90
Having Sympathy 92
Shaking Hands 94
Speaking Nicely...96
Saying Salaam 98
Joking..100

CHILDREN AND AKHLAQ

TABLE OF CONTENTS

1. Jealousy

2. Kindness

3. Respecting Parents & Teachers

4. Honesty

5. Stubbornness

Hadith 1: JEALOUSY

Imam Ali (a):

اَلْحَسَدُ يَأْكُلُ الْحَسَنَاتِ كَمَا تَأْكُلُ النَّارُ الْحَطَبَ

Jealousy destroys good deeds just like fire burns wood.

Ghurar al-Ḥikam, Ḥadīth #1891

Let's Discuss!

- What is jealousy? Jealousy is when we see someone else's blessing and want Allah to take it away from them and give it to us. One way to avoid jealousy is to be happy and pray for others. When we feel happy for others, Allah is happy with us, too!
- Remember that Allah has granted each of us many blessings. Instead of focusing on what we **don't** have, we should be thankful for all the gifts He has given us. If we like something someone else has, we can pray that Allah blesses us with that, too!
- Can you come up with a list of blessings in your life? Remember to say Alhamdulillah for each blessing!

COLOR

DISCUSS

How is the little girl not following the hadith?

_____

_____

_____

KINDNESS

Hadith 2

Prophet Muhammad (s):

مِنْ حَقِّ الْمُؤْمِنَ عَلَى الْمُؤْمِنِ إِذَا مَرِضَ أَنْ يَعُودَهُ

When another believer is sick, you should visit him.

Al-Kāfī, Vol. 2, Ḥadīth #88

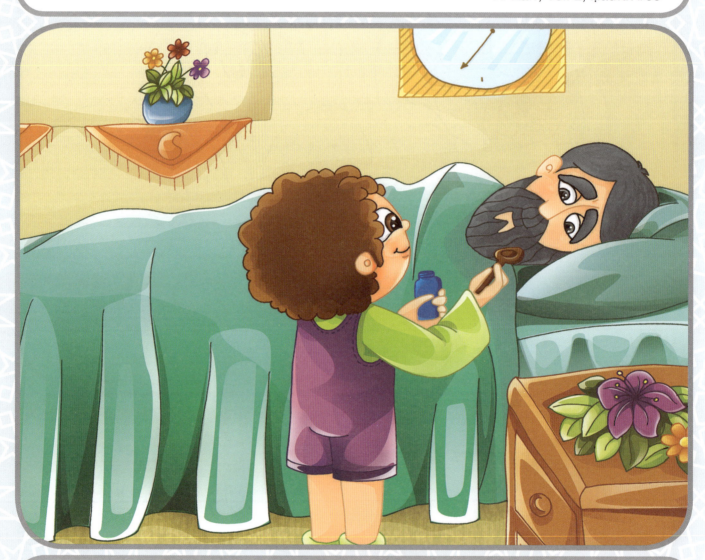

Let's Discuss!

- Why is it good to visit sick people?
- If someone around us is feeling sick, visiting and being kind to them will make both Allah and that person happy!
- What are some ways we can show kindness to someone when they're feeling sick?
- Can you think of a time you showed kindness to someone who was sick?
- How would you want others to treat you when you're sick?

SPOT THE DIFFERENCE

Find and circle 7 differences between the two pictures and discuss.

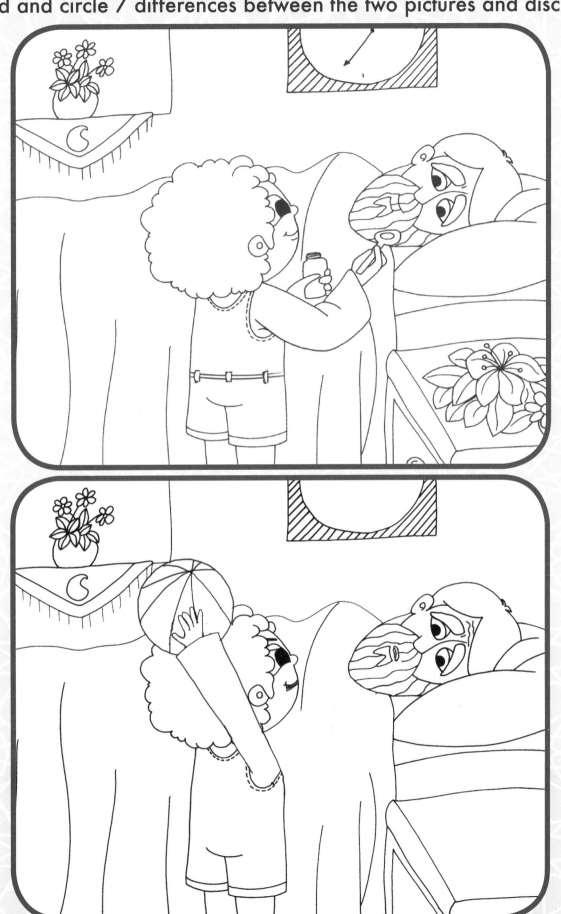

Hadith 3: RESPECTING PARENTS & TEACHERS

Imam Ali (a):

قُمْ مَجْلِسِكَ لِاَبِيْكَ وَ مُعَلِّمِكَ وَاِنْ كُنْتَ اَمِيراً

Respect your father and teacher by standing up (when they enter the room), even if you are a king.

Ghurar al-Ḥikam, Ḥadīth #2341

Let's Discuss!

- What are some ways we can show respect to our parents and teachers?
- Allah teaches us to respect and honor our parents and teachers by standing up when they enter the room and greeting them with a smile!
- Remember, our parents and teachers work very hard so we can be successful in life. One way we can show our appreciation and respect for them is by standing up to greet them, even if we are playing or feel tired. Even if we reach a super high status, like a king, the status of our parents is still higher!
- Today, try standing up and greeting your parents and teachers when they enter the room and see how they react!

COLOR BY NUMBERS

1 - Blue
2 - Green
3 - Pink
4 - Dark Brown
5 - Purple
6 - Light Brown

DISCUSS

How is the little girl not following the hadith?

_____

_____

_____

HONESTY

Hadith 4

Imam Ali (a):

اَلصِّدْقُ أَمَانَةٌ

Truthfulness is trustworthiness.

Ghurar al-Ḥikam, Ḥadīth #5258

Let's Discuss!

- What is truthfulness? What is trustworthiness? Truthfulness is when someone tells the truth, and trustworthiness is when people rely on you.
- When we are honest and tell the truth, people will trust us more.
- Sometimes, it might be really hard to be honest, but we should remember that when we do the right thing, Allah will always help us!
- How does it feel when someone lies to us?
- How can telling one lie lead to telling more lies?

COLOR AND CROSS

Color the picture that is following the hadith and cross out the one that isn't.

DISCUSS

How is the little boy not following the hadith?

_____

_____

_____

Hadith 5: STUBBORNNESS

Imam Ali (a):

اَللَّجَاجُ يَعْقِبُ الضُّرَّ

Bad things can happen to a stubborn person.

Ghurar al-Ḥikam, Ḥadīth #8950

Let's Discuss!

- What does it mean to be stubborn? A stubborn person is one who refuses to listen to others.
- How can bad things happen to someone who is stubborn?
- Sometimes, we really want to do something, but it might be that this isn't good for us. It is also possible that we don't want to do something, but this thing could be really good for us. For example, if this little girl refuses to take her medicine, she won't feel better. It's a good thing she's not being stubborn and is taking her medicine!
- Can you remember a time you were stubborn? How did it make others feel?

COLOR

DISCUSS

How is the little girl not following the hadith?

_____

_____

_____

_____

CHILDREN AND BEHAVIOR

TABLE OF CONTENTS

1. Mistakes

2. Rushing

3. Trying Our Best

4. Doing Good Deeds

5. Trustworthiness

Hadith 6 — MISTAKES

Imam Ali (a):

اِذَا زَلَلْتَ فَارْجِعْ

Whenever you make a mistake, accept and correct it.

Ghurar al-Ḥikam, Ḥadīth #884

Let's Discuss!

- What does it mean to accept our mistakes? How should we react when we accidentally do something wrong?
- If we are unsure about something, we should ask our parents or teachers, so they can help us before we make a mistake.
- If we do make a mistake, that's okay. We can ask for help and try to fix it!
- When we accept our mistakes, we learn what is right and wrong, so that we can make better choices in the future! Allah loves it when we learn from our mistakes!
- Can you remember a time when you made a mistake? How did you react?

SPOT THE DIFFERENCE

Find and circle 7 differences between the two pictures and discuss.

21

Hadith 7: RUSHING

Imam Ali (a):

اَلْعَجَلُ نَدَامَةٌ

Rushing will lead to [bad choices] that will end in regret.

Ghurar al-Ḥikam, Vol 1, P. 34

Let's Discuss!

- What does regret mean? How can rushing lead to regret?
- Regret is when we do something and then later wish we had not done it. Sometimes, when we do something too quickly, we can make a mistake and then regret it.
- Have you ever made a mistake because you were rushing and should have been more careful?
- Try this next time you want to rush: count to three before doing that action. This will help you to slow down so you don't have any regrets!

COLOR BY NUMBERS

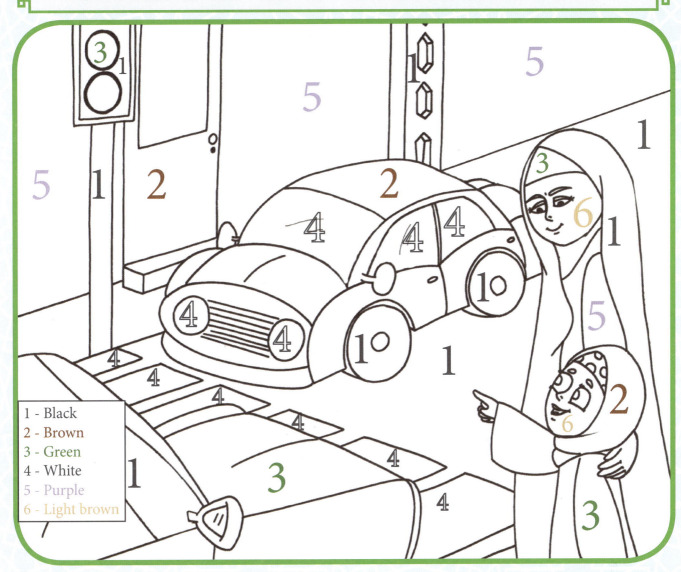

1 - Black
2 - Brown
3 - Green
4 - White
5 - Purple
6 - Light brown

DISCUSS

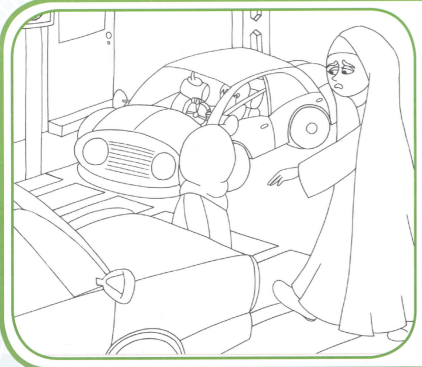

How is the little girl not following the hadith?

_____
_____
_____

23

Hadith 8: TRYING OUR BEST

Imam Ali (a):

قِيمَةُ كُلِّ إِمْرِئٍ مَا يُحْسِنُهُ

The value of a person is based upon how hard they try.

Nahjul Balāghah, Ḥadīth #81

Let's Discuss!

- Why is it important to try our best at everything we do? Even if we feel we aren't good at something, trying our hardest will help us improve and sharpen our skills! Remember, hard work helps us perfect our actions!
- We should always pray that Allah gives us the ability to be good at everything we do!
- Next time you have a difficult task to do, try putting in your best effort and see how it turns out!

COLOR AND CROSS

Color the picture that is following the hadith and cross out the one that isn't.

DISCUSS

How is the little boy not following the hadith?

_____
_____
_____

Hadith 9: DOING GOOD DEEDS

Prophet Muhammad (s):

اَلدَّالُّ عَلَى الْخَيْرِ كَفَاعِلِهِ

A person who guides others toward goodness will receive many blessings.

Al Kāfī Vol. 4, P. 27

Let's Discuss!

- How can we guide others to goodness? What are some examples?
- Just like the little boy is helping his two friends make up, we can also help others do good things!
- When we see someone needs help, we should do what we can to help them. InshaAllah, Allah will reward us for it!
- Can you think of a time when someone helped you make a good decision?
- Make a list of some good deeds you can do to help others!

COLOR

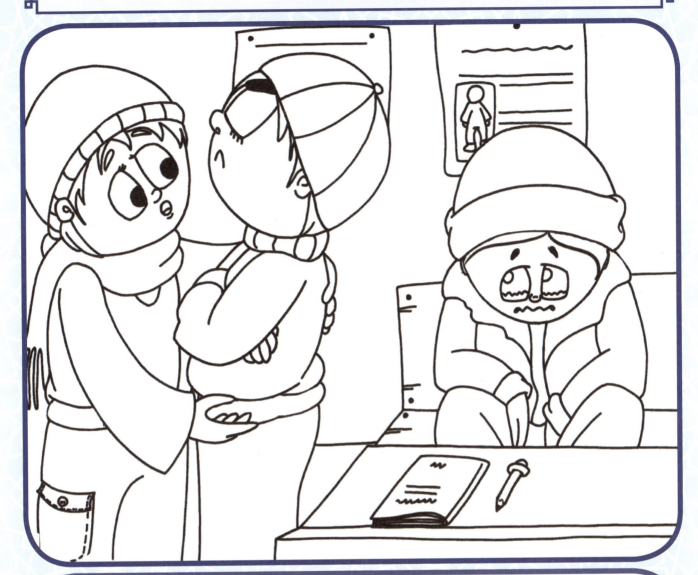

DISCUSS

How is the little boy not following the hadith?

_____

_____

_____

Hadith 10: TRUSTWORTHINESS

Imam Ali (a):

عَلَيْكَ بِالْأَمَانَةِ

Be Trustworthy!

Tasnīf, 251

Let's Discuss!

- What does it mean to be trustworthy?
- Being trustworthy means that we keep our promises, are reliable, and tell the truth. These are all qualities that Allah loves!
- What are some ways that we can become more trustworthy?
- If we lose someone's trust by not keeping our promises, what can we do to regain their trust?

SPOT THE DIFFERENCE

Find and circle 7 differences between the two pictures and discuss.

CHILDREN AND MANNERS

TABLE OF CONTENTS

1. Reputation of Muslims

2. Forgiving Others

3. Removing Dislike

4. Showing Love

5. Keeping Good Friends

Hadith 11: REPUTATION OF MUSLIMS

Prophet Muhammad (s):

مَنْ رَدَّ عَنْ عِرْضِ اَخِيْهِ الْمُسْلِمِ وَجَبَتْ لَهُ الْجَنَّةُ اَلْبَتَّةَ

Paradise is wajib on someone who protects the reputation of a Muslim.

Thawāb ul-ʿĀmāl, P. 145

Let's Discuss!

- What does the word reputation mean? Our reputation is what other people think of us and how they see us.
- Remember, a good friend helps protect their friend's reputation and doesn't share their mistakes with others!
- We should always share good things about others! When we do this, Allah will also help others think nicely about us.
- Today, try telling someone one good thing about two of your friends.

COLOR BY NUMBERS

1 - Green
2 - Brown
3 - Yellow
4 - Pink
5 - Blue
6 - Light Brown

DISCUSS

How is the little boy not following the hadith?

_____
_____
_____

Hadith 12: FORGIVING OTHERS

Prophet Muhammad (s):

إِذَا جُنِيَ عَلَيْكَ فَاغْتَفِرْ

When someone makes a mistake, forgive them.

Ghurar al-Ḥikam, Ḥadīth #6505

Let's Discuss!

- What does it mean to forgive someone? When we forgive someone, this means we let go of hard feelings, like anger, pain, or sadness, when someone is mean to us.
- Allah loves it when we forgive each other quickly!
- If someone apologizes to us, we should say "I forgive you" or "That's okay," and not stay upset about what they did.
- Think of someone who made you upset. What should you do to make the Imam of our time happy?

COLOR AND CROSS

Color the picture that is following the hadith and cross out the one that isn't.

DISCUSS

How is the little boy not following the hadith?

_____
_____
_____

35

Hadith 13: REMOVING DISLIKE

Imam Ali (a):

اُحْصُدِ الشَّرَّ مِنْ صَدْرِ غَيْرِكَ بِقَلْعِهِ مِنْ صَدْرِكَ

If you remove dislike from your heart, it will disappear from the other person's heart, too.

Nahjul Balāghah, Ḥadīth #178

Let's Discuss!

- What does it mean to dislike someone?
- If we dislike someone, we can pray to Allah to help remove our bad feelings and replace them with good ones. Allah will help cleanse our hearts and the heart of the other person as well, inshaAllah!
- Sometimes, it might take a while for the negative feelings to go away, but that's okay. We should be patient and try to make good choices during this time. We shouldn't show someone we don't like them by being mean to them, not sharing, or doing other unkind actions.
- Today, try praying for someone who you may have been unkind to.

COLOR

DISCUSS

How is the little girl not following the hadith?

_____

_____

_____

Hadith 14: SHOWING LOVE

Imam as-Sadiq (a):

اِذَا اَحْبَبْتَ رَجُلاً فَاَخْبِرْهُ

If you love someone, tell them.

Al-Wasāʾil, Vol. 8, P. 435

Let's Discuss!

- Who are some people we can show our love to? How can we show our love and care for our parents, grandparents, and siblings?
- There are many ways to show someone we love them: helping them, writing cards, using kind words, giving flowers, hugging them, and so on!
- Did you know when we show others love and kindness, Allah will show us even more love and kindness?
- Today, make a card telling someone how much you love them!

SPOT THE DIFFERENCE

Find and circle 7 differences between the two pictures and discuss.

39

Hadith 15: KEEPING GOOD FRIENDS

Prophet Muhammad (s):

اَلْجَلِيْسُ الصَّالِحُ خَيْرٌ مِنَ الْوِحْدَةِ وَالْوِحْدَةُ خَيْرٌ مِنْ جَلِيْسِ السُّوءِ

Being alone is better than being with a bad person, and being with a good person is better than being alone.

Biḥār ul-Anwār, Vol. 74, P. 84

Let's Discuss!

- Why it is important to have good friends?
- Having and being around good friends is a gift of Allah. Good friends help us become the best versions of ourselves!
- A bad person is someone who tries to get us to do bad things. We should ask our parents if someone is a good or bad friend!
- Think of a friend who always helps you. What are some of his or her good qualities that you can learn from?
- What are some activities that you like to do with your friends? Make a list, and try to get through all of these activities with your friends!

COLOR BY NUMBERS

1 - Brown
2 - Blue
3 - Red
4 - Yellow
5 - Green
6 - Light Brown

DISCUSS

How are the little girls not following the hadith?

_____
_____
_____

CHILDREN AND GUESTS

TABLE OF CONTENTS

1. Guests and Angels
2. Serving Guests
3. Respecting Guests
4. Making Room for Others
5. Whispering

Hadith 16: GUESTS AND ANGELS

Prophet Muhammad (s):

كُلُّ بَيْتٍ لَا يَدْخُلُ فِيهِ الضَّيْفُ لَا تَدْخُلُهُ الْمَلَائِكَةِ

Angels will not enter a house in which guests are not welcomed.

Summary of Mizān al-Ḥikmah, Ḥadīth #3774

Let's Discuss!

- Why do you think guests are so special?
- Guests are very special because Allah has said that they bring blessings into our homes!
- What can we do to make guests feel welcome in our home?
- We should serve, feed, and be kind to our guests.
- Angels love visiting homes where these good deeds happen!
- The next time you have guests in your home, make a card or welcome note for them, so they feel extra special!

COLOR AND CROSS

Color the picture that is following the hadith and cross out the one that isn't.

DISCUSS

How is the little girl not following the hadith?

_____

_____

_____

45

Hadith 17: SERVING GUESTS

Prophet Muhammad (s):

اَقِرُّوا الضَّيْفَ

Serve your guests.

Ghurar al-Ḥikam, Ḥadīth #2030

Let's Discuss!

- What are some things we can serve our guests?
- When guests visit our home, we should offer them the best of what we have! We should share our toys, serve them our favorite snacks, and speak to them kindly.
- When we give our guests the best of what we have, our guests feel honored and Allah is happy with us.
- The next time you have guests in your home, help your parents prepare a special snack or meal for them. This will make your guests feel special and give you the chance to earn extra rewards from Allah!

COLOR

DISCUSS

How is the little boy not following the hadith?

_____

_____

_____

47

Hadith 18: RESPECTING GUESTS

Imam Ali (a):

مَنْ كَانَ يُؤْمِنُ بِاللهِ وَالْيَوْمِ الْآخِرِ فَلْيُكْرِمْ ضَيْفَهُ

If you believe in Allah and the Day of Judgment, you should honor and respect your guests.

Jami-ʿul-Akhbār, P. 377

Let's Discuss!

- What does it mean to honor and respect our guests?
- We can honor and respect our guests by spending time with them and making them feel very welcome in our homes.
- When guests visit our homes, we should spend time with them and speak kindly to them.
- We know that our good deeds toward our guests will be rewarded by Allah on the Day of Judgment!
- What are some fun things you can do the next time guests visit your home?

SPOT THE DIFFERENCE

Find and circle 7 differences between the two pictures and discuss.

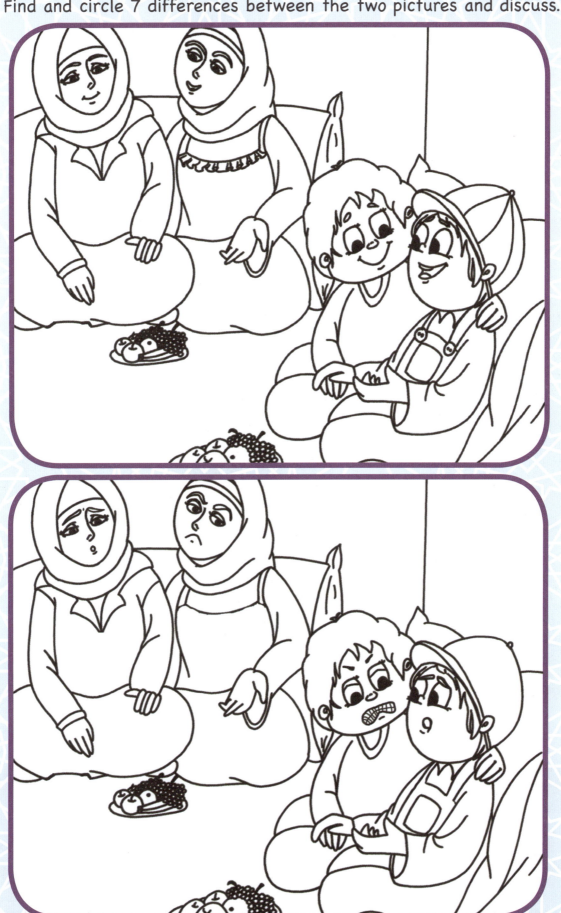

49

Hadith 19: MAKING ROOM FOR OTHERS

Prophet Muhammad (s):

تَوَسَّعْ لَهُ فِي الْمَجْلِسِ

Make room for others in a gathering.

Nahjul Faṣāḥa, Ḥadīth #1293

Let's Discuss!

- Why do you think making room for our guests is so important? How does this make our guests feel?
- One way to help our guests feel welcome is to give them a special place to sit and welcome them with a big smile.
- If there are a lot of guests and not too much space, how can we make room for our guests?

COLOR BY NUMBERS

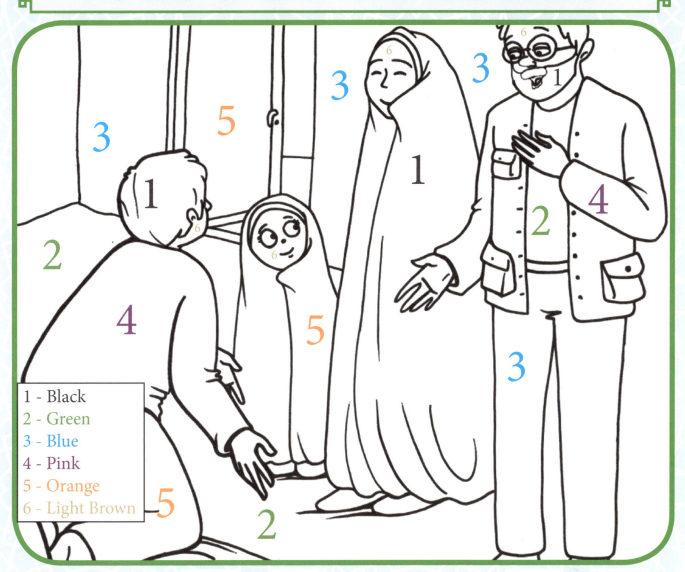

1 - Black
2 - Green
3 - Blue
4 - Pink
5 - Orange
6 - Light Brown

DISCUSS

How is the little girl not following the hadith?

_____

_____

_____

WHISPERING

Hadith 20

Prophet Muhammad (s):

وَلَا تَنَاجَ مَعَ رَجُلٍ وَاَنْتَ مَعَ آخَرَ

When you are with people, it is not polite to whisper in one person's ear.

Ghurar al-Ḥikam, #884

Let's Discuss!

- What does whispering mean?
- Why can it be impolite to whisper in front of others?
- Our words and actions are very powerful and can either help or hurt others. We should be very careful not to tease or make fun of others by whispering.
- If we need to tell a friend something that we can't share with others, then we should say it at a later time.
- How might our friends feel if we whisper in front of them?

COLOR AND CROSS

Color the picture that is following the hadith and cross out the one that isn't.

DISCUSS

How is the little girl not following the hadith?

_____

_____

_____

CHILDREN AND HYGIENE

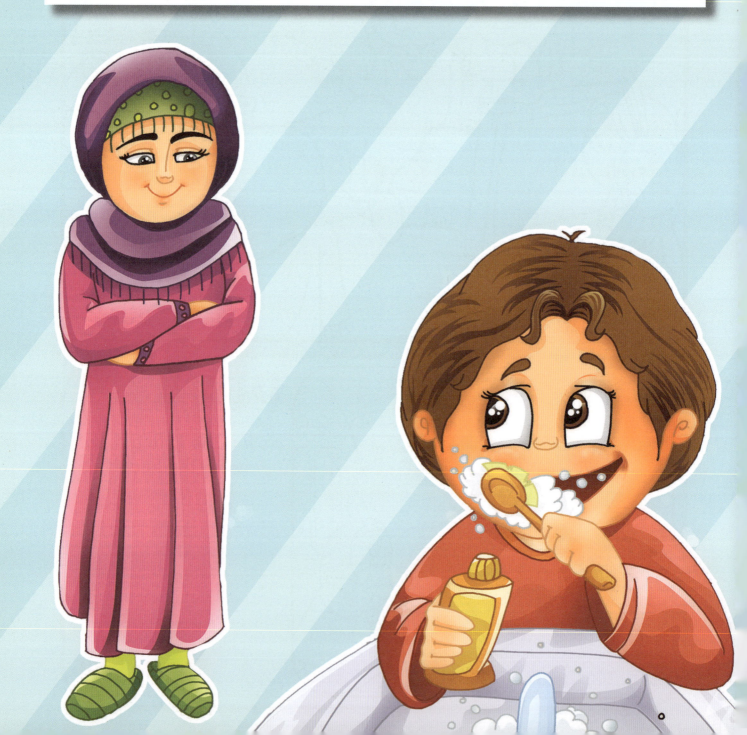

TABLE OF CONTENTS

1. Washing Our Hands

2. Brushing Our Teeth

3. Oversleeping

4. Messiness

5. Washing Clothes

Hadith 21: WASHING OUR HANDS

Imam as-Sadiq (a):

اِغْسِلُوا اَيْدِيْكُمْ قَبْلَ الطَّعَامِ وَبَعْدَهُ

Always wash your hands before and after you eat.

Maḥāsin, Vol. 2, P. 1594

Let's Discuss!

- Why is it important to wash our hands before and after eating?
- It is important to keep ourselves clean because Allah loves cleanliness. It is also important to wash our hands to get rid of germs before eating.
- What is the best way to wash our hands properly? We should take our time and make sure to use soap to clean them properly.
- Today, try washing your hands before and after every meal you eat!

COLOR

DISCUSS

How is the little boy not following the hadith?

_____

_____

_____

Hadith 22: BRUSHING OUR TEETH

Prophet Muhammad (s):

اَلسِّوَاكُ مَطْهَرَةٌ لِلْفَمِّ وَ مَرْضَاةٌ لِلرَّبِّ

Brushing cleans your mouth and strengthens your eyes.

Al-Kāfī, Ḥadīth #4

Let's Discuss!

- Why is it important for us to brush our teeth every morning and every night?
- When we go to the dentist, what does he or she look for in our teeth?
- If our teeth are not clean, what does he or she do?
- Prophet Muhammad (s) made sure to keep his teeth clean all the time. He would even brush his teeth before praying salaah!
- Did you know that we get special rewards for brushing our teeth?
- Let's practice brushing our teeth carefully and at least twice a day!

SPOT THE DIFFERENCE

Find and circle 7 differences between the two pictures and discuss.

59

Hadith 23: OVERSLEEPING

Imam as-Sadiq (a):

كَثْرَةُ النَّوْمِ مَذْهِبَةٌ لِلدِّينِ وَالدُّنْيَا

Oversleeping will hurt your faith and take away the blessings of this world.

Al-Kāfī, Vol. 5, P. 84

Let's Discuss!

- What is oversleeping? Oversleeping is when we sleep more than we need to.
- How many hours should we sleep every night? We should sleep until we are well-rested, about 7-9 hours.
- Why might oversleeping be bad for us?
- If we oversleep, we might miss salaah, feel lazy to do our work, or waste time!
- There's a saying that goes, "Early to bed and early to rise makes a man healthy, wealthy, and wise!"
- Practice sleeping early tonight so you can wake up nice and early tomorrow!

COLOR BY NUMBERS

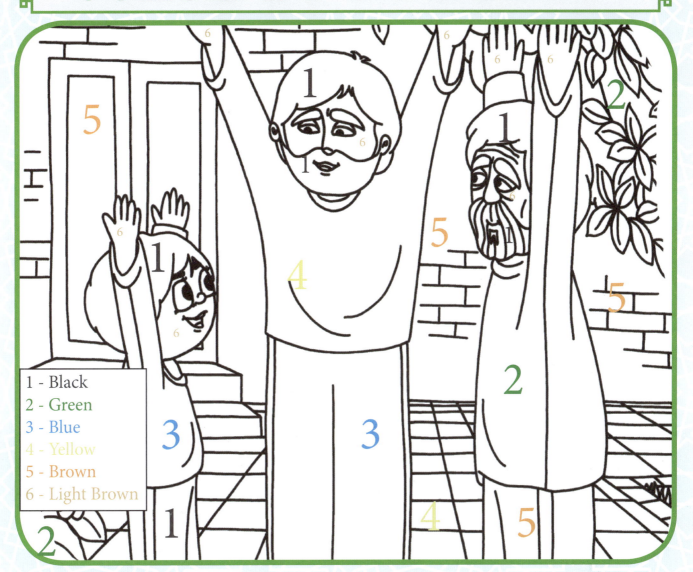

1 - Black
2 - Green
3 - Blue
4 - Yellow
5 - Brown
6 - Light Brown

DISCUSS

How is the little boy not following the hadith?

_____

_____

_____

Hadith 24: MESSINESS

Prophet Muhammad (s):

اِنَّ اللهَ تَعَالىٰ يُبْغِضُ الْوَسَخَ وَالشَّعَثَ

Allah dislikes messiness and disorganization.

Nahjul Faṣāḥah, Ḥadīth #741

Let's Discuss!

- What do the words messiness and disorganization mean?
- Messiness and disorganization are when a person is untidy or does not have things in order.
- What are some places that should always be kept organized? What happens if, for example, the grocery story is messy and disorganized?
- How do we feel when we know where everything is? How does organization help us finish our work faster?
- Today, try to clean and organize your room. See how much better you feel afterwards!

COLOR AND CROSS

Color the picture that is following the hadith and cross out the one that isn't.

DISCUSS

How is the little girl not following the hadith?

_____

_____

_____

63

Hadith 25: WASHING CLOTHES

Prophet Muhammad (s):

اِغْسِلُوا ثِيَابَكُمْ وَتَنَظَّفُوا

Wash your clothes to keep your body and soul pure.

Kanzul ʿUmmāl, Vol. 6, P. 640

Let's Discuss!

- Why is it important to wash our clothes?
- It is very important to keep our clothes clean so we can feel clean and happy, and the people around us enjoy being around us.
- How do you feel when you get to wear new and pretty clothes?
- How do you feel when your clothes get dirty or someone else is wearing dirty clothes?
- The next time your parents are doing laundry, try to help them!

COLOR

DISCUSS

How is the little boy not following the hadith?

_____
_____
_____

CHILDREN AND NUTRITION

TABLE OF CONTENTS

1. Feeding the Needy

2. Eating Less

3. Chewing Properly

4. Eating Hot Food

5. Protecting the Environment

Hadith 26: FEEDING THE NEEDY

Imam al-Baqir (a):

إِنَّ اللهَ يُحِبُّ اِطْعَامَ الطَّعَامِ

Allah loves those who feed the needy.

Biḥār ul-Anwār, Vol. 71, P. 361

Let's Discuss!

- Why is it important to feed the needy? Who are the needy people?
- When we feed those who are in need, it shows that we care about Allah's creations. Allah likes it when we help and care for people who need our help. After all, all our blessings are from Allah, so we should share them with others, too!
- Can you think of any stories about the Ahlul Bayt that teach us to feed the needy?
- Try making a sadaqa box today! Everyday, you can add in a little bit of money. When the jar is full, you can take your jar to the masjid and they will give the money to the needy!

COLOR BY NUMBERS

1 - Black
2 - Green
3 - Blue
4 - Brown
5 - Yellow
6 - Light Brown

DISCUSS

How is the little boy not following the hadith?

_____
_____
_____

Hadith 27: EATING LESS

Imam Ali (a):

اَقْلِلْ طَعَاماً تُقْلِلْ سَقَاماً

Stay healthy by eating less.

Ghurar al-Ḥikam, Ḥadīth #2336

Let's Discuss!
- Why should we be careful not to eat too much?
- When we eat too much food, we usually feel lazy and tired.
- Eating healthy foods helps us take care of the precious bodies Allah has given us. If we eat unhealthy food or overeat, our bodies will feel tired and we may not have energy to do good deeds.
- Many ahadith tell us that we should stop eating before we feel full. This will help us not to overeat.
- The next time you have a meal, remember not to stuff yourself!

SPOT THE DIFFERENCE

Find and circle 7 differences between the two pictures and discuss.

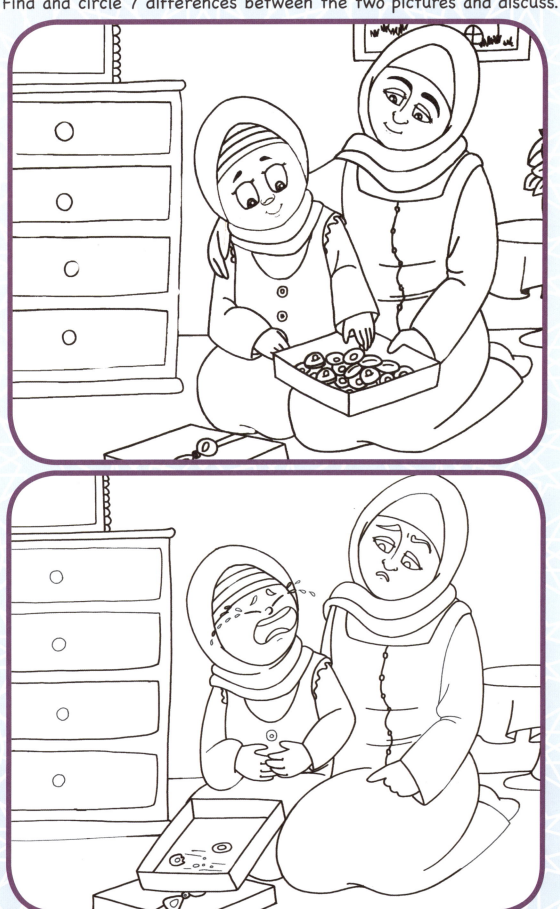

Hadith 28: CHEWING PROPERLY

Imam Ali (a):

جَوِّدِ الْمَضْغَ

Always chew your food properly.

Biḥār ul-Anwār, Vol. 62, P. 267

Let's Discuss!

- Why is it important for us to chew our food properly? What might happen if we don't chew it properly?
- Our teeth help break down the food we eat, so our bodies can easily digest the food.
- It is important to chew our food so that we enjoy what we eat, and this also makes the job of our stomachs easier. Chewing properly also helps us not to choke on our food.
- So, remember to slow down and chew your food properly, even when you are really hungry!

COLOR AND CROSS

Color the picture that is following the hadith and cross out the one that isn't.

DISCUSS

How is the little boy not following the hadith?

_____

_____

_____

Hadith 29: EATING HOT FOOD

Prophet Muhammad (s):

لَا تَأْكُلِ الْحَارَّ حَتَّىٰ يَبْرُدْ

Do not eat hot food until it cools down.

Qisār ul-Jumal

Let's Discuss!

- What happens if we eat food that is too hot?
- Hot food can burn our mouths and hurt our stomachs. We should wait until it cools and not blow on our food to cool it down.
- When we blow on our food, we also blow germs, which can be harmful to our bodies.
- What are some other ways you can cool off your food?

COLOR

DISCUSS

How is the little boy not following the hadith?

_____

_____

_____

Hadith 30: PROTECTING THE ENVIRONMENT

Imam as-Sadiq (a):

لَا تَقْطَعُوا الثِّمَارَ فَيَبْعَثُ اللهُ عَلَيْكُمُ الْعَذَابَ صَبّاً

Do not ruin fruit trees because it will have bad results.

Mīzān al-Ḥikmah, Vol. 2, P. 1410

Let's Discuss!

- Why should we be careful not to ruin trees?
- Allah has created trees to help us and keep our air clean. Some trees give us fruits, too! If we destroy fruit trees, we will not be able to eat the tasty fruits that are blessings from Allah.
- Trees are also homes to animals, like birds and squirrels, and we shouldn't destroy animals' homes.
- What are some ways you can help save trees? Hint: reduce, reuse, recycle!

COLOR AND CROSS

Color the picture that is following the hadith and cross out the one that isn't.

DISCUSS

How is the little girl not following the hadith?

_____

_____

_____

CHILDREN AND SPIRITUALITY

TABLE OF CONTENTS

1. Helping the Oppressed

2. Blessings from Allah

3. Success

4. Humility

5. Good Children

Hadith 31: HELPING THE OPPRESSED

Imam Ali (a):

اُنْصُرُوا الْمَظْلُوْمَ

Always help the oppressed.

Bihār ul-Anwār, Vol. 91, P. 101

Let's Discuss!

- What does the word 'oppressed' mean?
- Someone who is oppressed is not treated fairly, and it makes them feel unhappy and uncomfortable.
- Imam Ali (a) has told us to always help people who are being treated unfairly.
- We should always try and help those who are oppressed around the world. If we cannot, the least we can do is pray for them.
- Tonight, when you make du'a, remember to make special du'a for all the oppressed people around the world!

COLOR BY NUMBERS

1 - Black
2 - Green
3 - Blue
4 - Brown
5 - Yellow
6 - Ligjht Brown

DISCUSS

How is the little boy not following the hadith?

_____

_____

_____

Hadith 32 BLESSINGS FROM ALLAH

Imam Ali (a):

اَلْمُؤْمِنُ يَحْتَاجُ اِلَى تَوْفِيقٍ مِنَ اللهِ وَقَبُولٍ مِمَّنْ يَنْصَحُهُ

A mo'min needs tawfeeq from Allah and should accept advice from others.

Tuḥfatul ʿUqūl, P. 457

Let's Discuss!

- What is tawfeeq?
- Tawfeeq is a special gift from Allah that helps us and gives us energy to do good deeds.
- When we do good deeds, we receive more tawfeeq from Allah. Doing more good deeds gives us lots of rewards, like doors opening for us in jannah!
- What are some good deeds you can do to get more tawfeeq from Allah?

COLOR AND CROSS

Color the picture that is following the hadith and cross out the one that isn't.

DISCUSS

How is the little girl not following the hadith?

_____

_____

_____

83

Hadith 33

SUCCESS

Imam Ali (a):

اَبْعَدُ النَّاسِ مِنَ النَّجَاحِ الْمُسْتَهْتِرُ بِاللَّهْوِ

The least successful people are those who waste time.

Ghurar al-Ḥikam, P. 460

Let's Discuss!

- Why is it important for us not to waste our time?
- Time is very special. We are only given 24 hours a day, and once we lose that time, we can never get it back.
- Time is like money. We need to use it to do good deeds so that we can have nice things in jannah.
- Try making a schedule for yourself, so you can see how you will use your time wisely and earn rewards for jannah!

COLOR

DISCUSS

How is the little girl not following the hadith?

_____

_____

_____

HUMILITY

Hadith 34

Imam Ali (a):

عَلَيْكَ بِالتَّوَاضُعِ

Always be humble.

Biḥār ul-Anwār, Vol. 75, P. 119

Let's Discuss!

- What does the word humble mean?
- To be humble means to speak politely, help others, and not show off.
- What is the opposite of humble? The opposite is being arrogant and showing off.
- Our Prophets and Imams were so humble that even people who did not like them would feel safe around them and ask them for help.
- How might others feel if we show off? Do we want to make anyone feel bad?
- When you feel like showing off, you should remember who gave you all the talents you have: Allah! Instead, you should thank Him.

SPOT THE DIFFERENCE

Find and circle 7 differences between the two pictures and discuss.

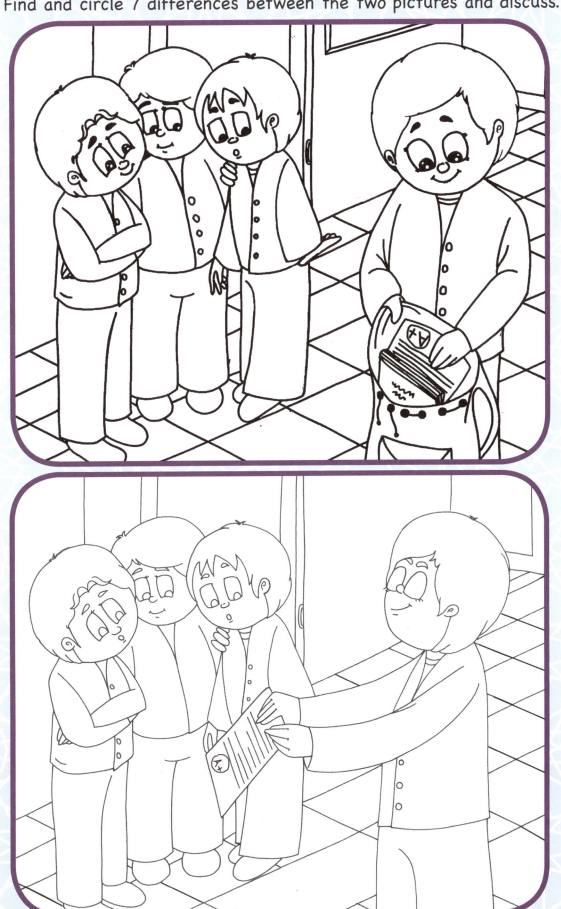

Hadith 35: GOOD CHILDREN

Prophet Muhammad (s):

اِنَّ الْوَلَدَ الصَّالِحَ رَيْحَانَةٌ مِنْ رَيَاحِيْنِ الْجَنَّةِ

A good child is like a flower amongst the flowers in heaven.

Uṣūl al-Kāfī, Vol. 6, P. 3

Let's Discuss!

- What are some qualities of a flower? How would you describe a flower?
- Just like flowers are beautiful, a person with good akhlaq is also like a beautiful flower who has a good effect on others.
- If we have good manners and respect, help, care for, and share with others, everyone will respect us, but more importantly, Allah will be happy with us!
- Try drawing a flower. On each petal, write down a quality you can have so that you are like a beautiful flower!

COLOR BY NUMBERS

1 - Purple
2 - Green
3 - Blue
4 - Brown
5 - Yellow
6 - Ligjht Brown

DISCUSS

How is the little girl not following the Hadith?

_____
_____
_____

CHILDREN AND UPBRINGING

TABLE OF CONTENTS

1. Having Sympathy

2. Shaking Hands

3. Speaking Nicely

4. Saying Salaam

5. Joking

Hadith 36: HAVING SYMPATHY

Imam Hasan al-Askari (a):

لَيْسَ مِنَ الْأَدَبِ اِظْهَارُ الْفَرَحِ عِنْدَ الْمَحْزُونِ

It is not good manners to be happy in front of someone who is sad.

Tuḥaful ʿUqūl, P. 489

Let's Discuss!

- Why should we try not to be happy in front of someone who is sad?
- It is not good akhlaq to show happiness when someone is sad because it might make the other person feel that we don't care about them or their feelings. This is called having sympathy.
- If we feel sad, how would we want others to treat us?
- We should be sensitive when someone is sad and not be extra happy around them.
- Can you think of some ways you can cheer up someone who is feeling sad?

COLOR AND CROSS

Color the picture that is following the hadith and cross out the one that isn't.

DISCUSS

How are the little boys not following the hadith?

_____
_____
_____

Hadith 37: SHAKING HANDS

Imam Ali (a):

اِذَا لَقِيْتُمْ اِخْوَانَكُمْ فَتَصَافَحُوا

When you see your friends, shake their hands.

Khiṣāl, Ḥadīth #633

Let's Discuss!

- Why is it good to shake hands with our friends?
- Allah loves it when we greet each other by shaking hands! This shows that we trust and respect the other person.
- Can you think of different times when we shake hands with other people?
- We shake hands when we see a friend, after salaah, and with the Imam of salaah.
- Today, practice shaking hands with everyone you see!

COLOR

DISCUSS

How is the little boy not following the hadith?

_____
_____
_____

Hadith 38: SPEAKING NICELY

Imam as-Sadiq (a):

كُونُوا لَنَا زَيْناً وَ...قُولُوا لِلنَّاسِ حُسْنًا

Make us (Allah and the Ahlul Bayt) proud of you and speak nicely to people.

Anwār fī Ghurar il-Akhbār, Ḥadīth #943

Let's Discuss!

- Why should we speak to others nicely? How will this make the Ahlul Bayt (a) proud?
- Allah likes it when we are nice to others. Our Prophets and Imams always spoke nicely to others, even to those who spoke to them rudely.
- Can you think of any stories where the Ahlul Bayt (a) were kind to people who treated them rudely?
- We are the flagbearers of the Ahlul Bayt (A) and represent the Muslims, so we should be extra kind, just like our role models.
- How can you speak more kindly to others?

SPOT THE DIFFERENCE

Find and circle 7 differences between the two pictures and discuss.

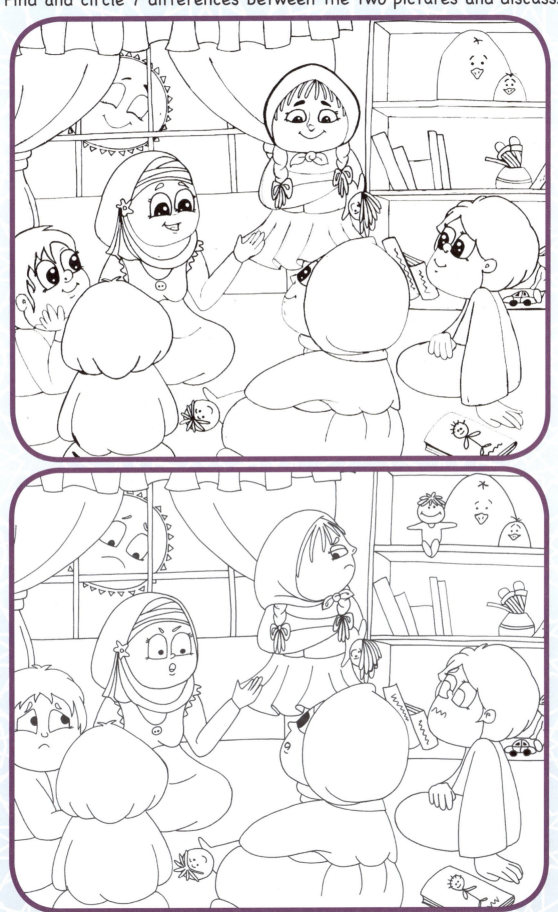

97

SAYING SALAAM

Hadith 39

Prophet Muhammad (s):

اَلسَّلَامُ اِسْمٌ مِنْ أَسْمَاءِ اللهِ تَعَالَى فَأَفْشُوهُ بَيْنَكُمْ

Salaam is one of Allah's names, so practice saying it with each other

Mishkat al-Anwār fī Ghuraril-Akhbār, Ḥadīth #1135

Let's Discuss!

- What does the word 'salaam' mean?
- Salaam means peace. When we say salaam to someone, we are actually saying that we will treat this person kindly and peacefully.
- The person who says salaam first gets the most thawaab or reward.
- When are some times that we should salaam to other people?
- Practice saying salaam to your parents when you wake up in the morning and give them a nice hug!

COLOR BY NUMBERS

1 - Green
2 - Brown
3 - Yellow
4 - Pink
5 - Blue
6 - Light Brown

DISCUSS

How is the little boy not following the hadith?

_____
_____
_____

Hadith 40: JOKING

Imam al-Baqir (a):

اِنَّ اللهَ عَزَّوَجَلَّ يُحِبُّ الْمُدَاعِبَ فِي الْجَمَاعَةِ بِلَا رَفَثٍ

Allah likes people who joke with friends without hurting others.

Al-Kāfī, Vol. 2, P. 663

Let's Discuss!

- Is joking good or bad?
- Jokes are a good way to have fun with friends. The Imams (A) taught us that it is good to joke.
- If our joke hurts someone's feelings, then it is not a joke; that is called teasing and bullying. We should never make jokes about someone else.
- We are all brothers and sisters in Islam and should love and respect each other.
- Can you come up with a good joke you can share with your friends?